# The Heart Is Another Name For God

A Metaphysical Journey
to Life's Purpose
(Yin and Yang)

Renee Pittman

Copyright © 2013 Renee Pittman
All rights reserved.

ISBN-13: 978-1-7374060-6-8

Mother's Love Publishing
and Enterprises

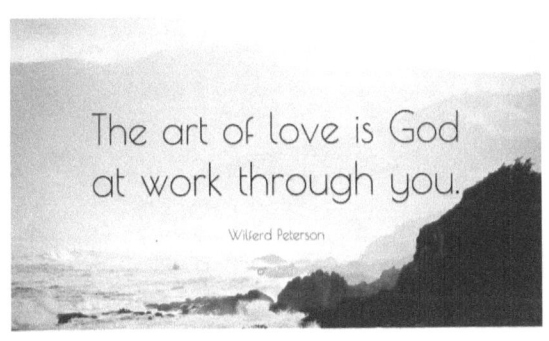

## **DEDICATION**

To my Dear *Milani and Miru*.
"Welcome to the world!"

## TABLE OF CONTENTS

Chapter One: Dreaming ........................................................ 1

Chapter Two: Lotus Flower .............................................. 13

Chapter Three: Superconscious ....................................... 23

Chapter Four: Ego .............................................................. 35

Chapter Five: The Concept of Fear ................................. 49

Chapter Six: The Concept of Oneness ........................... 58

Chapter Seven: Fifth Dimension Consciousness .......... 75

Chapter Eight: Global Change ........................................ 88

Chapter Nine: The Universal Church of God ............. 101

Chapter Ten: Nobody Told Me The Road would
              be Easy ..................................................... 105

The heart is a symbol of God's boundless and passionate love for humanity…

— Herbert Cooper,

"God supplies the contrast to our limitations, liabilities, and losses. He turns our expectations upside down, blows our minds, and transforms our hearts with the ways he loves us, protects us, provides for us, and redeems us."

**CHAPTER ONE**

# Dreaming

I dreamed I was encircled in light.

I called upon the Universal Light Force to guide me. I asked that only the highest energy of love manifest.

A warm energy then entered the room. I then saw myself moving forward walking down a path.

No matter what is happening around me, I continue walking. I am not worried that I am not going in the right direction.

There is a calm peace within.

A Monarch butterfly lands on my shoulder, lingers for a moment, then flutters off into the brightness of the day bringing the message of hope through transformation and regeneration. A Monarch butterfly in particular is a sign that you are on the right path to achieve your goals.

I get the message and am overjoyed.

I then begin to understand why life has taken both negative and positive experiences to move me forward now in the right direction. I step into my calling on this planet.

The experiences on my path, like the Lotus emerging from mud have taught me this. The hills and valleys of my struggles have also strengthened me preparing me. The outcome of it all good, bad, and ugly is that I am stronger, wiser, and better, so much better. Realizing this, counting it all joy I keep moving with a sense of wonder.

I realize from the darkest times that we are all in God's hands and are all being held up by a powerful, underlying foundation, and mighty unconditional love. Although did not see it at times, oblivious, forgetting that it is there, it is with us always and never forgot me. We are never separated from our Creator as its highest creation.

We are one.

This is the great lesson of polar experiences on the physical plane. Sadness, pain, heartbreak, sorrow, brings light mingled as time passes with joy and hope, bringing forth the present as a gift of wisdom. Awareness is transformed into light. Light ultimately becomes our foundation for Spiritual Wealth.

More valuable than gold, Spiritual Wealth then advances the infinite soul's continuous progression on the journey.

I realized that every answer of which I have been searching has always been on my path. I learn that God lives in the Heart as my heart warms.

It makes perfect sense now. Humanity is *illuminated* by this global, wonderful force and we are evolving together. We are infinite immortal beings.

Every single soul, on Earth School, will continue movement towards enlightenment, in various stages, the objective. It cannot be stopped. It cannot be any other way. It is the meaning of evolution. It is as true today as it was yesterday or since the beginning of time.

What if this is a chosen reality in which we dwell, of which some argue a holographic existence we created with our minds. If so, the reason for our existence and our Being is by grand design. We are valuable to the whole no matter who. What if we made a contractual agreement for it ALL? If so, don't fret, after all you signed up to live it.

Did we choose specific experiences which would bring forth the light in which our Soul seeks to fuel the ascension to greater spiritual heights?

As I am walking my path, I pause for a moment, look around, and see the struggles of others going through various stages of development.

Sometimes it's not a pretty sight. I want to call out to them and say, don't worry, "All things are working together for good" but I cannot. They must live and learn also.

I see lives that appeared to have insurmountable odds and hardships, who have overcome. I think to myself, as a toss and turn feeling their pain and uncertainty. "What brave souls" if they chose this reality. If this concept is true, they have decisively chosen this path to Light. They knew when making the selection, that certain experiences, on the physical plane, will accelerate closeness to the light of God and greater understanding?

And, learn that after hardship many, instead of lingering in the fruitless deeds of darkness choose to remain in Light for the rest of their lives. Hardship's itself has played a Divine role for, and revelation of, the Master's plan.

I get it.

The Divine presence leaves no one behind. Nothing can or ever will prevent *Divine Order* from manifestation and progression. It must unfold. The Universal Light Force emanating from the Most High knows only singularity of purpose.

I feel the warmth of the Sun on my face redirecting me back to my path as my dream state continues. I began walking again.

My path is drawn to me. Every piece of the puzzle that I need keeps falling into place before me, step by step, at my feet on the trail. When I need the next experience, it falls perfectly in line. One Jade stone after another is placed in front of me.

Gemstones are symbols of strength and endurance.

The Jade stone symbolize Divine revelation as a symbol of good fortune, good health, wisdom, and Universal Attunement. They are the link between the Spiritual and mundane. With a new understanding, they now line up for me to purposely walk on.

All I must do is just keep walking.

Life has always had direction I see clearly now.

However, I realize that there were times when a stone landed at my feet and my foot had to be purposely placed upon it through lack of in sight. If not, how else could I grow, learn, and all experiences unleash discernment?

There were times in my naivety, that if any door appeared open on my path I walked through it. Silly me I think now, but then realized, it is all good.

I pass many doors now as I walk, selective, aware after learning. The doors that are off my path do not remain open for entrance any longer. They quietly are shutting in my face as I approach saying you don't want to go that way again.

They were not the right doors for me and no longer, serve a purpose. They were not the right way. They were there to lead me off my path, and if they could would again.

The right doors open effortlessly and because of this I walk through them with ease into the glistening light.

I have no doubts. I am sure when I reach them.

Directly in front of me, falling into place is a guiding light ushering me forward. The beautiful stones continue to fall. I tread intentionally upon the creamy sensation beneath my feet. Soft and at times slippery, I must maintain my balance.

As I walk I have in my hand a bag of seeds.

The seeds were harvested from everything that I have learned, endured, and experienced both good and bad.

As I look inside the heavy bag, the seeds glow with love originating from the Universal Light Force.

I begin sprinkling the seeds to the right and left of my path. Birds are coming and eating the seeds. Flowers and trees are growing and blossoming. I am amazed at the love of God.

I hope in my heart the seeds I plant will lead to greater understanding and new beginnings for others too. I think. I hope that my life will be an example and help others. I hope that I can and will make a difference.

I want to be a beneficial presence on this planet. I can't think of any other valid reason for being here when I look back except for this.

One thing is certain I have walked my path steady. I have stumbled and fallen but have always gotten up and continued walking. This was although battered, bruised, and even limping at times in great pain.

Nothing causes me to stray now.

I realize that Light is not at the end of the tunnel that it is, and always has been all around me permeating my Soul.

I began humming softly, then quietly reciting one of the many affirmations that have helped me to make it through some of the toughest times in my life. I recite:

*I am light, glowing light, radiating light, intensified light. God consumes my darkness transmuting it into light.*

*I am the focus of the Central Sun.*

*Flowing through me is a crystal river of light that can never be qualified by human thought or feeling.*

*I am an outpost of the Divine…*

I remember many times that these simple words brought comfort and joy and helped me continue.

The illuminating rays are mesmerizing beautiful surrounding me now.

I see the green healing light with the Golden Light of Grace infused within the wonderful Universal Light Force.

Intensity and warmth radiate through every part of my being. I look to see if the same light is shining on the seeds, the birds, and others walking their paths.

It is!

It is reflected in an array of colors, shapes, and sizes, sprouting, blossoming, as the darkness gradually dissipates. Life is renewed with many new beginnings in our lifetimes.

Birds with broken or clipped wings, and plants that were wilted by intense storms, begin to fly, stand tall, erect, reborn, and are breathtaking beautiful radiating an inner beauty.

I look to the right and two beautiful Flamingos wings are instantly healed and they both immediately fly off towards the Central Sun.

The Central Sun is the source of the all-pervading, all knowing omnipotent, "I AM." It is the location where Heart integrates with body, mind, Spirit and Soul in Oneness within the Master Cosmos.

The Master Cosmos are the cause of all matter, consciousness, and existence.

It is the center for release of light. It is a place that basks in enlightenment, and knows only compassion, joy, harmony, peace and love. It is the centralized concentration of the gift of the Christ Consciousness.

Suddenly I hear an angelic voice say, "Follow the water; follow the water, the water has a sign for you."

Over and over and over, this gentle voice of consciousness repeats, "Follow the water. Follow the water. Follow the water."

I do not know at this point what it means. I do not see any water as I peer forward squinting my eyes. It must be further ahead. What is the message? What will I learn when I arrive at the water? One thing is certain, it will be revealed to me, as all things have at the appointed time.

The powerful Universal Light Force is like a current, or a ripple. If I try to turn around, or go in another direction, or even step backwards, it will not allow it now. I have come too far.

This warm energy continues to nudge me forward.

In complete trust, my path has taught me, trust, faith, and to never doubt a "Divine Plan" for it all.

Yes, I like many, am only human, and was briefly blinded, but "I can see clearly now, the rain is gone! I can see all obstacles in my way."

As long as I align myself with the real purpose for existence, to help and serve, and focus on creative thought, word and deed by originating from the goodness of Heart, and apply this in all action, I connect self-to-self, and get closer and closer to God, my heart's desire.

I connect with my real self, which is an emanation of, and the likeness of God. Our original being is love.

Many times, as I walk I am tempted to pick up my pace, walk faster or even run. But I am patient. It is said that patience is a virtue for good reason.

Slowly but surely, I will make it. Slowly but surely, I will get there, and all in due time. I look forward to the surprise to the next adventure.

Look how far I have come already I remind myself. I am moving at the right pace.

No matter what the illusions or perceptions of life, in the polar state of negative and positive, not only for me, but for you as well, there is an unchangeable and deeply rooted foundation grounded in pure love and at the Heart of all matter.

Mother Earth is simply the playground and more importantly, as a whole and collectively for life as a place to learn to love and experience it.

We are on a steady path together.

We continue to move forward and in the direction of Divinity. After all we are the Mother and Father God's creations. Created in Love and all that really matters.

Love allows forgiveness. It heals all. It rejuvenates. It motivates. It brings goodness, blessings, and joy just as God's unconditional love does.

Allow yourself to focus and be motivated by the *goodness* of Heart. It is contagious and a gift to share, pay it forward.

In unity, let us advance this universal concept of consciousness originating from love in the heart of the ability to create beauty on this planet. I believe we will then begin to accept, and live the true meaning of our existence, a reality of love, vital for survival of all life, as we step into our rightful places as Co-creators with the omnipresence Creator working through our hearts and willingly being used to advance the betterment of humanity.

Deep within the *"Super Conscious"* lies the truth.

It is hidden by what we are programmed to believe on this material plane, and by those seeking to control humanity and stop the ascension which enlightens then abolishes the control matrix and paradigm.

It is where the *Light* of *Truth* resides and the awareness of which we will return according to our beliefs and actions when it is all said and done. Doing good attracts good even during trials.

With this recognition, through the storms, and chaos of life, I do not dismay. I understand that step-by step, as Co-creators, we partook in the design of our consciousness. Without consciousness we would not exist.

All life and activity are the result of polarity which awakens consciousness, creates friction within polar and various states, then provides knowledge. This results in the inherent, innate desire to evolve, to grow, and ascend focused on the *Light of God* our desire and by design.

There are no exceptions.

So, my Dear Reader:

> *Be joyful in hope, patient in affliction, and faithful in prayer.*
> ---Roman 12:12

And remember,

**Beyond Belief ...It's All Good**

**CHAPTER TWO**

# Lotus Dream

The Lotus flower is one of the most ancient and deepest symbols of our planet dating as far back as Creation. It is said that the Lotus was the first flower God created.

According to one creation myth, it was a giant Lotus which first rose out of the watery chaos at the beginning of time. For this giant Lotus, the Sun itself rose on the first day.

The timeless beauty of the Lotus is that it grows in muddy slime at the bottom of a pond or stream and rises above the surface to bloom in remarkable and pure beauty each day.

At night the flower bows, retreats, whispering "Namaste" to the God within all life, folds its petals, closes and sinks underwater to the warmth of its muddy, bed. At dawn it again rises, then makes its journey or ascension again, and reopening.

Untouched by the impurity of its beginnings, the Lotus symbolizes the plight of the human spirit and the purity and blossoming of the human spirit through hardship and conscious awakening.

The Rhizome is the heart of the Lotus.

A "rhizome, in philosophy has no beginning or end; it is always in the middle, between things, inter-being, "intermezzo," balanced. Because it is rooted in the mud the rhizome can survive and re-germinate for thousands of years.

This pattern of growth signifies the progress of the soul from the primeval mud of materialism, through the waters of experience, and into the bright sunlight of enlightenment and spiritual development.

The Lotus is recognized all over the world, by many religions, because of the symbolism of its beginning and its singular purpose of journey.

Each and every day, is a day of renewal.

The Christian alternative to the Lotus flower is the White Lily which relates to Mary as Queen of Heaven.

Heaven is a non-literal place that the mind created in remembrance of where it originated and where it desires to return. It is a distant memory of a place of harmony, contentment and complete bliss. In the illusion of this experience, it is a subconscious longing.

When we choose Earth school, we locked away, in a golden treasure chest, all other previous experiences so that our sole purpose here will not be influenced.

However, we do at times experience a state of euphoria on our journey and it can be very powerful.

It is an awakening, a recognition, and remembrance of a profound love we feel lingering around us.

The Water Lily over time has come to signify both fertility and purity although this definition is based on a common misbelief that the Lotus and Water Lily are the same flower. They are not.

It is said that Archangel Gabriel carried the Lily of the Annunciation to the Virgin Mary.

*Blessed are the pure in heart,* said Jesus, *for they shall see God.*

I believe it true that the pure in heart will see God by electromagnetic frequency attraction. We and also attract good or evil.

Through the darkness, the mud itself plays a pivotal role in the recognition of almighty God.

We begin to understand that the Lotus has been assisted by the mud in the beginning. We begin to understand that the Lotus could not have made it or prevailed without it.

Make no mistake between the Water Lily and the Lotus.

The Lotus is antediluvian, dating back eons. Many religions recognize the spiritual message of this specific flower and the connection to enlightenment.

In Buddhism the flower, symbolizes purity, enlightenment and spiritual unfolding. It is symbolic of the awakening to the real spiritual significance of life itself. It brings a message of beauty and peace not derived from material possessions. It brings an understanding of the purpose of suffering which starts the healing process.

Perhaps, this meaning is closest to the factual essence of the flower.

For the message of the Lotus flower is a factual spiritual revelation that the experiences of life give knowledge of a Divine reason on every level.

In this dynamic, the contributions of many circumstances are revealed as good, and all having great value. It gives an understanding that great beauty unfolds and can originate from the metaphor of slime and muddy experiences.

It is a message of endurance, strength, courage, and above all, a powerful message of hope. As the flower makes its journey and continues to bloom day after day, for thousands of years and many, many, lifetimes, unstoppable. We too awake each day continuing our soul's progression.

On our journey, there are many new births and new beginnings in many forms which are not connected to an actual physical death.

We are reborn anew in our perceptions, our beliefs, and vision for our lives at different stages.

All are forms of new growth, regeneration and renewal, which are essentially imbedded through trial and error.

In Egyptian mythology, the Lotus symbolized creation and rebirth as well.

In ancient Egypt, the sun was worshipped as the source of life. This is through its life-giving energy and ability to grow life and equated symbolically, to God.

By comparison, it is the same light of the Sun that motivates the Lotus to make its journey refueled and empowered.

Another interpretation is the Hindu belief.

All interpretations are slightly similar, however, not only does the Lotus symbolize divinity and fertility, in Hinduism, but it also is a symbol of wealth, knowledge, and triumph over adversity.

What greater triumph than to prevail and gain greater *insight*. This type of wealth is the highest form of prosperity that can be acquired.

It is not superficial and leaves its imprint within for eternity. The wealth of which it brings is not determined by any physical illusion of happiness, joy by possessions, grandeur, houses, cars, or a bank account.

Real true Spiritual Wealth brings a profound gift.

It is an awakening to the reality that our Masterful Creator has many, many, more miracles and wonders to show us as our consciousness expands.

It is an awakening to the reality of the essence of God as a comforter, nurturer, and rescuer, and restorer in our most difficult times. It is our teacher and friend. It is a loving parent allowing the mud of experience to do its work.

True also in Hinduism, the Lotus represents long life, and honor. But again, good fortune can be measured as contentment or any altruistic effort.

This sacred flower, and the powerful position it holds in many religions for eons and cultures is a symbol of the true purpose of life.

Remember it ascends from the mud, at the *bottom* of the pond. Its steady ascension from the bottom up, inch by inch, motivated by an invisible force and blind determination magnifies the ultimate redemption of humanity.

The beauty revealed in the flower once breaking water is unsurpassed. What is amazing is that it unfolds in pristine beauty without even a speck of mud on it or even a blemish. The mud nourished it, sustained its growth, promoted its development and strengthened it for its purpose as support.

The parallel of evolution of the human spirit, or the journey of the soul, and this magnificent flower are the same.

However, unlike the flower, we appear temporarily blinded to the truth from our muddy experiences as human beings, or the reality of the beneficial affect resulting from our manifestation on the physical plane and focus on materialistic ideals.

Unlike the flower, the mud of hardship, sorrow, and pain, is viewed as an enemy to growth and development in life.

Due to materialistic beliefs, life can appear to be somewhat of a curse and experiences without merit, importance or valuable and especially without lots of money though our programming on the material plane.

Struggles are not recognized for what they truly are. They are powerful opportunities to blossom.

We are unaware that like the Lotus a biological and physiological clock has been set at creation by our Creator and placed within our own Heart's desire. This biological clock of conscious awareness is incorporated into our very DNA.

Our struggles in life are the mud and activating force nudging us forward. It is the same as a specific blooming time, at the right time and right season for flowers.

The message of this flower is the connection of life to the omniscient. If the desire of this flower, singularly, is to seek light and this desire is instinctually implanted within the flower genetically, at creation, by an all-knowing God, then why would it not be also implanted in God's highest creation destined for, higher consciousness and higher truths?

Why would not the same God also program individuals and humanity as a whole, through various beginnings, conditions, trials, to be naturally inclined instinctually, intuitively, by this life force to move upwards?

The *truth shall set you free* from the prison of wrong and illusion perceptions of what life is really about.

The Lotus is free when it breaks water and blooms never separated from the Rhizome.

We must recognize the mud for what it truly is. It is a beautiful foundation which brought forth ultimately beauty.

When we understand this we become free, separating ourselves from the illusions of delusions of a one-sided materialist path or separateness or disconnection in this world from Light. With this understanding, we embrace life as having a totally different goal, greater meaning and greater purpose.

The flower without forethought obeys its calling and so will you and I.

Though, unlike humanity, which is God's highest creation, the Lotus, has no complaint, or conception of its humble beginnings as anything other than what is necessary for growth and development to achieve its goal.

The mud for the Lotus is the sacred, life sustaining, and life giving, foundation for its destiny.

When awakened the human experience on this plane revealed in the journey it will become exactly what it is, and always has been meant to be, an unfolding in the magnificence of God's light, and recognition of a connection never broken.

It does not matter, who, where you start, or what has happened in your life, your color, shape, or size, etc. Nor does circumstance, environment, or a perception of failure, or your having no real value. You have no real power to stop what unconditional love has around you always within reach.

Never forget that it is the muddy foundation of the Lotus which steadies it, and held it in place. Never forget that the mud is no less as important as the flower itself.

Understand that the mud of pain makes you stronger. The mud of tears makes you wiser. And, the mud of heartbreak, pain and sorrow serve to make you better.

So, thank the mud and know that you will continue to be renewed on the immortal journey of your soul.

Know that Light is really a word which is short for "enlightenment" and that enlightenment is the ultimate goal for all.

**CHAPTER THREE**

# Superconscious

*The awareness of life existence is simply the result of consciousness.*

The Superconscious mind contains within itself the ability, to create, anything and everything, that can be conceived within it. And, the possibilities are endless.

Involution is the awakening within our deeper self.

Evolution is a universal concept of experience which can be attributed to not only humanity as a whole, but worldly events, characterized by evolution in general. For example, evolution is defined as:

*"The inherited characteristics of biological populations over successive generations.*

*Evolutionary process give rise to diversity at every level of biological organization, including species, individual organisms, and molecules such as DNA and proteins"* …

Involution (esoteric) is described as:

Note that the term involution refers to different things depending on the writer.

In some instances, it refers to a process that occurs prior to evolution and gives rise to the cosmos, in others an aspect of evolution and still others a process that follows the completion of evolution in the human form.

Involution prompts a journey deep within seeking access to the location of super consciousness.

Involution sets the stage for evolution and together, in partnership they result in a unified conscious awakening. In the polar state of this dimension balance is the key.

The physical plane itself is ruled by perceived limitations and perceptions of the five senses which define our reality in 3D.

The five senses are that of taste, touch, sight, smell and hearing. In reality, they are all one in the same. There is really only one sense. It is the sense of feeling. All other senses are different forms of this sense.

To see, hear, touch, smell or taste is to feel.

The five senses are limited because they appear as separate experiences to the mortal mind.

The mortal mind is our intellect which compiles information from the outside world. As a result, the senses have the ability to report wrong information back to our feelings.

For example, two people having a similar experience, seeing, hearing, tasting, touching or smelling the same thing can report their feelings as completely different based on their individual reality.

Why does one person have a taste for a certain food, activity, etc., and another find it distasteful?

The Sixth Sense is that of intuition or Extra-Sensory Perception.

Our thoughts can also be counted as our Sixth Sense.

Western culture suggests that the sixth sense is something supernatural. However, in Eastern cultures the sixth sense is defined simply as the activities of the mind, such as thinking and opinions.

The Seventh Sense is that of our emotions.

Our intuition is most powerful when you are able to feel and understand what you are feeling in our emotions.

The sixth and seventh sense work together. Your seventh sense is there as a helper for the sixth sense.

The author of the *Enlightened Feelings* website writes: `

Evolution has provided all living things with a range of senses to interpret and interact with the world. Senses are controlled by the same part of the brain that stores memory. That is no co-incidence, as remembering sensations or experiences allow all living things to move toward pleasure and avoid pain or danger.

The Eight Sense is the awakening.

It is the elevated conscious state in which we seek to understand reality, and answers of why. How and why the world exists? Why are we really here? Who is God? Why are things the way they are? What is our role in Divine Reality? And, more importantly, how can we make the world a better place?

The Eight Sense is where realization shows up and releases a desire to create a beautiful presence on this planet. The eight sense in essence connects the dots. The eight sense is also awareness of a higher ideal of progression, and the universal unification under God and not man.

"Unlike the five senses or the sixth and seventh sense, the eighth sense requires a conscious choice to access an aspect of the mind not confined to space and time.

It is metaphysical.

Symbolically this supra-mind can be represented by the joining in an act of love for the brother sitting next to you. It also includes a joining with the idea of Jesus or the Holy Spirit.

It is the desire of the mind to extend beyond the confines of the human condition. The miracle always brings joy because it is literally the escape from prison, escape from the prison house of the body, at the mercy of aging, disease and fear"

"The Eight Sense and Your Awakening," writes Alden Hughes, in an article for the Miracle Healing Center.

Many doctrines describe the eight senses according to the environmental reality of consciousness.

For example, in the Eastern culture of Buddhism, there are six basic senses and not five as in Western culture. They are defined as gates, *doors*, organs or roots.

In Buddhism, the sixth sense "mind" is defined as an internal sense organ which interacts with sense objects which includes perceptions, feelings, and even sense impressions and volition.

The eight sense is the awakening of the super conscious. It defines the false reports of the five senses on the material plane as false and gives meaning.

The eight sense is so powerful that it dissipates the illusion of any inability to co-create our reality and therefore brings inner peace. Essentially, we understand that sky is truly the limit. The eight sense is an unwavering truth. It is a truth which is always, without exception, final and absolute.

The eight sense truth awakens the knowledge of God's unconditional love for humanity no matter what perception the five senses had reported.

It also reveals the false reporting of fear, as an illusion of the five senses. Fear itself has played a pivotal role in reducing humanity to surviving at any, or at all cost, and as a tool promoting separation, death and war.

When we connect with higher intelligence, I believe our values shift. We begin to understand that we do not need objects to be content, find joy or peace in life.

The eight sense dissipates the five sense reality that life is worthless without material trappings. I say trappings because, the pursuit of these objects solely, without equal pursuit of spiritual advancement create imbalance and without the resulting joy many learn after pursuit.

The desire, motivated for these things, can become so overpowering that the mortal mind can temporarily blocked the awareness of super consciousness, and awareness of our connection to the One.

The superconscious is the location deep within our inner self connected to the pineal gland or what was once called the Third Eye. It is that which the so-called controllers of this dimension hope to keep closed.

It is the Central Sun within. It is where all knowledge, from lifetime to lifetime exists and thrives.

We are *Spiritual Beings* temporarily housed in a physical manifestation which we call a body. The doctrine of rebirth or incarnation is the key to understanding how long-term human growth and development is designed to take place supposedly.

The concept of reincarnation is based on two self-evident truths that require no proof, and of which are a universally accepted principle in most doctrines.

They are:

a. The soul or spiritual self-existed before physical birth and will continue to live after death and is thereby immortal.

b. Consciousness is infinite and its evolution extends into eons.

c. The journey of the spiritual self is on a constant mission of self-realization and seeking a more perfect expression of its Divine potential through incarnations or ascension.

d. Each life, of many lives, are steps taken on the pilgrimage back to the Creator or Edenic Bliss.

During the period between life to life experiences, the soul assimilates the lesson learned from the previous life just past.

The essence of the previous life is then stored in the super conscious for use in future incarnations subconsciously.

The super conscious holds the answers. It knows the reason for existence, why there is good and evil and the truth that death is merely a passing because the within the super conscious, the "Third Eye" is wide open.

It is the equalizer, and honors all contributions to the Master's plan, whether big or small, knowing each contribution has equal value and that Karma is part of the growth process and also a part of unconditional love.

Be aware, that a wrongful determination can serve to keep the soul trapped in a false reality which is a resulting limit of five sense reporting.

Karma is a naturally occurring state of polar experiences where experiences are designed for spiritual growth.

James Allen writes in *As a Man Thinketh,*

*Every man is where he is by the law of his being, the thoughts which he has built into his character have brought him there, and in the arrangement of his life there is no element of chance, but all is the result of a law which cannot err.*

*This is just as true of those who feel "out of harmony" with their surroundings as of those who are contented with them.*

Also, life is a process designed for self-correction.

The Material or Physical Plane is described as:

The physical plane or hyperplane, physical world, or physical universe, in emanationist metaphysics such as are found in Neoplatonism, Hermeticism, Hinduism, and Theosophy, refers to the visible reality of space and time, energy and matter: the physical universe in Occultism, (occult meaning merely hidden knowledge or esoteric,) that which is hidden cosmology.

Is the lowest or densest of a series of planes of existence or hyperplanes that are said to be nested.

May I add that the "lowest of densest" is key. Lowered frequencies create death, destruction, hatred, harm, chaos, suffering and peril and more heinously and typically hides.

Emanationist metaphysics is defined as Absolute Reality which is the essential limitless, perfect, nature of things.

As with all Universal Law, when born into the physical plane of materialism, life itself becomes the polar opposite state to our real identity.

In the polar universe both negative and positive experiences are working together to advance growth and bring the only ultimate reality of truth.

Involution or eight sense awakening and awareness is ignited when there is a desire to connect with our higher self, the goals of the Creator and desire to live life in sync with this powerful force for good.

When this happens, we are fueled with the knowledge that infinite possibility has always existed, which we were blinded beforehand due to five sense erroneous reporting or clever manipulation and influence.

On the path of life to redemption, there is nothing more valuable than gaining an understanding of the purposeful rising, step-by-step, of the immortal soul and the understanding that Karma cannot exist without incarnation. In this respect, all things are truly working together for good for those who love God! Chose you side wisely.

There is a vast difference in the definition of reincarnation and incarnation.

Reincarnation suggests that a soul can go backwards which is against Universal Evolutionary Law.

For example, a human soul cannot reincarnate as an animal in another life.

Incarnation defines forward movement and awareness that after reaching God's highest creation as human beings, there is only forward movement for continued advancement of the spiritual self.

Collective Karma is also a manner in which Karma operates and is designated for results at the collective level.

We are all individuals, it is true, but we do not live in isolation from others. Our thoughts and actions affect others, whether we recognize it or not.

On a daily basis, we can transfer positive energy and create a domino effect through this human connection as well as transfer negativity.

With this recognition, the "our" and the super consciousness can direct the personality and intellect for good only originating in the heart.

Eight Sense altruistic awakening leads to a kinder, forgiving and loving nature, and we then infuse this essence throughout the planet and the universe, seeking good, and only good, for goodness sake, and thereby creating the world we want to see.

Our journey is for us to look within, connect, awaken, become refined by the fire and to know that we were never truly separated and are factually connected to all in an unbroken chain to all life.

Superconscious revelations demand conscious awareness and bring hope and an endeavor to make all effort based on the fact that "We are here for God."

Make no mistake about it, we are intertwined socially, economically, culturally, and greatest of all Spiritually as shown by the image of energy emanating from a centralized powerful location and branching outward in many directions and in varying and different degrees and intensities.

Make no mistake about it; have no fear, *ALL* life is unconditionally loved through the powerful energy originating from omnipresent source of Light known also as *The Light of the World*.

God is the One life, one power, and One Spirit pushing outward from within. At times, we may feel disconnected or appear that we are, however we are not! It is impossible. Again, "All things are working together for good."

## CHAPTER FOUR

# Ego

In Mystery School initiations, the flame of the lamp represents the Ego, as a living, brilliant, changeless *Spark of Deity*.

The asbestos wick which ever feeds the flame, yet is never consumed, represents the immortal soul feeding the ego with, we now understand is the results of its experiences.

Tradition teaches that the androgynous (neither male or female) Ego, or "Spark of Deity" at the core of each soul, existed in an unconscious and blissful state of Eden or Edenic purity but was tempted to undergo involution into material form for the sake of acquiring consciousness through the symbolic knowledge of the Tree of Good and Evil.

'The spark of Deity' was then cast upon the muddy banks of the Delta (the material world.)

It is common knowledge that classic nations, as well as people of antiquity, believed in the doctrine that the soul once existed in a pure spiritual state, and that it was tempted to undergo involution into material form for the sake of acquiring knowledge, and must ultimately win its way back to paradisiacal bliss.

Had it not been for the ego's desire, the human soul would have remained in uncomplicated bliss but the desire is to connect with our higher self and our benevolent creator, the highest, God almighty.

One of the key words in the story of the symbolic fall of man is the word "tempted."

This word, not only should alert, but also caution, each of us to the power of ego and Ego's ability to create chaos, misrepresent, and hope to throw the Divine plan off course. But in truth, can it really if all is working together for good?

A wanton ego is capable, as we have seen, of directing the human soul or spiritual self, off a path and as far away from Divine intent as it can.

It is empowered by this believing it does not need any connection with God.

All great teachers have taught that in order to change the world we must first have change ourselves.

However, in order to change ourselves, ego, must become subservient to the will of Spirit and used only for the good and not strictly for Ego's selfish goals, and the desires of Ego alone.

In the biblical story of the Serpent, Adam and Eve appear to have been perfectly content in their blissful state in the beginning. This was until ego prompted them through temptation.

The effectiveness of temptation was founded on their belief that something was lacking or missing in their lives and that which the Serpent asserted truly was.

In Divine reality, we know there is no lack or limitation in progression. The Egos of both Adam and Eve then sought to be like God, which they already were by created in God's likeness.

However, in ego's case, the purpose, and the ultimate goal of ego is, and always has been, to actually be God by disconnection.

When considering this truth, it is not difficult to understand why ego in Arabic literally means Devil.

Ego by definition is a noun which describes a person's sense of self-esteem or self-importance: Ego is also described as the part of the mind that mediates between the conscious and the unconscious and is responsible for reality testing and the sense of awareness of self.

In simplest terms, ego means "I".

The problem arises when the concept of "I" separates itself from the Universal Light Force of God, "I AM."

Exodus 3:13 - And Moses said unto God, Behold, when I come unto the children of Israel, and shall say unto them, the God of your fathers has sent me unto you; and they shall say to me, what is his name? What shall I say unto them?

Exodus - 3:14 And God said unto Moses, I AM THAT I AM: and he said, thus shalt thou say unto the children of Israel, I AM hath sent me unto you.

The *Super Ego* concept originates in classical psychoanalysis emanating from Freud. It is kind of the "parent" we carry around with us, perhaps functioning through a personal belief of self- actualized Divinity conceived as separate.

Ego, super-ego and id., the place where ego and libido urges meet, make up the three components of the psyche in Freudian psychoanalysis.

The id contains the libido, which is the primary source of instinctual forces. The super-ego can stop you from doing certain things that your id may want you to do. Id knows no judgment of value. It knows no good or evil, no morality and is an instinctual *cathexes* or urge seeking discharge or release from the mortal mind.

The Medical Definition of *cathexes* is the investment of mental and emotional energy in a person, object, or idea, while another definition states that cathexes are lib-id-inal energy that is either invested or being invested.

The id is regarded as the reservoir of lib-id-o, the instinctive drive to create the life instincts that are crucial to pleasurable survival.

As a result, id becomes the energy behind consciousness which brings knowledge of existence creating both good or bad.

Alongside the life instincts came with the death instinct.

In reality, the hypothesis of the death instinct is the task in which purpose is to lead organic life back into the inanimate state of Edenic bliss as described earlier.

Freud also believed that the death instinct would thus seem to express itself, though probably, only in part, and egotistically as an *instinct of destruction* directed against the external world and other organisms through aggression.

In other words, seeking power selfishly for self- sake at the cost of others.

One of the most telling characteristics of ego is egos dedication to ego and only to ego.

More telling is the fact that ego, egotistically does not grasp that it operates on a lower vibration or lowered realm of consciousness.

As a cunning thief, ego will expertly rob you of real truth and light through total and complete deception by distorting your perception, cleverly, your reality and your senses.

A disconnected ego, does not want to acknowledge where strength and light truly originate because it believes itself the source.

God can be seen in miraculous acts, achievement, and amazing feats in life. However, ego's goal and purpose are to obliterate the real source of blessings and miracles and claim it as acts of its own.

Ego wants you to deny God's assistance, and even portray the illusion of mud misery, as the only reality and for you to believe that God caused this not for good and expansion.

It creates the confusion that your strength and everything you did was done all by yourself thereby successfully denying any connection to any Supreme power greater than yourself.

Ego manipulatively uses the fact that God's presence is unseen in our physical lives.

It is not difficult to understand why. Essentially, as stated, ego has always wanted to be God.

Within the human soul, ego can become the polar opposite of God's Spirit and thereby keep the personality in a constant, relentless, reckless state of spiritual warfare within itself.

As this battle rages, the human ideation must be to align these two polar opposite forces in balance, tame ego, and thereby revitalized the connection to the One and recognize the continuous advancement of the spiritual self.

As discussed earlier, polar states are a necessary dynamic designed to ultimately create KNOW-ledge through conflict. However, you must first thoroughly recognize that two opposite states exist before this awareness can create balance through the recognition itself. You have to be aware of a factual opposition.

The battle rages because ego does not want to become subservient to the *Spiritual Self* or in second place to the real spark of Deity of which it was designed to work with, because in its purest sense it is un-evolved.

It wants a light of its own and wants to be egotistically separated from the unification of the great I AM but the great ME.

There is an ongoing internal power struggle and conflict of interests as ego tries to continuously set itself up as God within, and in its vanity, does not believe there is anything wrong by dwelling under the absence of the true authentic Light.

Some of the characteristics, of many of ego are: destruction, greed, envy, jealousy, conceit, murder, arrogance, hate, superiority, conceit, vanity, war, fear and manipulation, etc., etc., etc. However, at the top of the list for ego is the desire and thirst for power, and the hope to ultimately control any and everything and everyone around it and God's creation

In order to do this, ego knows it must use and substitute darkness, by any means necessary through skillful misinterpretation of reality. There are several methods, for example, tell-a-vision is just one of many.

In reality, ego's superiority ideation is a well-disguised inferiority complex. The fact is, Ego was created by God but decided to separate and took only the hopeful Deity aspect of God as its own. Remember ego was there at conception and is symbolized in the story of creation as an adversary to God's will for humanity.

Ego has free will, as does all of God's creation.

I believe that "Free Will" is God's complete trust in the Holy Spirit within each of us revealing that ultimately light is more powerful than darkness and God's faith in the human Spirit's ability to guide us out of darkness.

It appears that ego was angry at its inception, from the very beginning, and vowed to change its position through influence.

Job 1:6-7

One day the angels came to present themselves before the lord, and Satan also came with them.

The Lord said to Satan, "Where have you come from?"

Satan answered the Lord, "From roaming throughout the earth, going back and forth on it.

How ego achieves this goal does not matter to ego. At best ego will step on many to glorify itself and shine in its synthetic light achieved typically through destruction. Ego operates and is motivated for power and only for power's sake alone.

Ego, as "I" is a Spark of Deity only, again, only when it is harnessed for good intent to make life and lives better.

However, so twisted is ego allowed to evolve in some by choice that it is so twisted that it actually calls evil good as well, and good evil.

Ego thrives on conquering people, is never satisfied, never happy, or completely fulfilled and after the challenge of the conquest arrogantly announces, "Look at me. See what I did, and, I did it all by myself" and moving right along hungry.

In the polarity of the universal experience, for every action, there is a separate but equal reaction also known as the Law of Cause and Effect.

Ego thrives as the polar opposite of humility, compassion, brotherly love, human kindness, altruism, and inner and outer peace.

The bible speaks clearly of Ego's capability of deception saying:

Isaiah 5:20 - Woe to those who call evil good and good evil, who put darkness for light and light for darkness, who put bitter for sweet and sweet for bitter.

Isaiah 5:21 - Woe to those who are wise in their own eyes and clever in their own sight.

The God Spirit does not seek to glorify itself and operates humbly in silence and quietly stands by watching.

Where ego has delusions of grandeur, Spirit is content in humility, service, gratitude and thanks, and basks in the *Light of God*.

Spirit was there at creation too. It knows ego well and understands ego's antics.

It knows that ego vainly believes that it has effectively pulled the wool over the eyes of God's creation or so it thinks, and actually does for an instant.

However, to ego's dismay it just cannot change what we really are.

Although ego is *always* relentlessly busy trying,

Spirit rests assured in authentic power emanating from good intention. Spirit is first and far most motivated by, and only by love, without exception.

So, loving is the Holy Spirit that it is even prepared to come in and clean up the wreckage ego leaves behind and even loves ego unconditionally knowing that there is a day of reckoning for Evil and it won't be pretty.

Spirit has learned through welcomed trial, and tribulation, that it can do all things, empowered by God who strengthens.

Founded in pure love, Spirit is long suffering, charitable, and due to this characteristic is actually amused by ego.

Spirit is not condescending, another characteristic of ego, and knows that equally God loves the saint as well as the sinner.

Spirit is aware that certain untruths can be the outcome of the misguided perception of egotism and that perception can manifest as darkness as Adam and Eve learned on their path it appears.

Spirit knows that in reality there is actually no darkness only the absence of light. Evil itself is the absence of good.

As the Sun sets in one location Light is always assured to rise in another.

In wisdom, Spirit knows that the concept of darkness is yet another of many necessary dynamics on the material plane. To see Light, and understand Light you must experience darkness to compare Light too.

Spirit knows that by design, the human soul cannot serve two masters and ultimately it will not. It knows that once a soul chooses to follow, "I AM the Light, the way and the truth," that it actually ignites the true spark of Deity within the heart and soul, and its true nature and connection.

So, although ego stands temporarily in opposition to the highest potential of the human soul at times, briefly, Spirit waits patiently, trusting, and knowing, that it will, eventually, ultimately be victorious.

It always has been.

Spirit's foundation springs from the spearhead of the *All-Knowing God Intelligence* permeating all.

In defense of ego, we must acknowledge that ego has its place and Divine role in the grand scheme of things by giving us choices.

Ego, for example, can help you to recognize God's reality through its very opposition and outcome.

However, understand that the goal is for ego to willingly submit to Spirit and completely surrender ALL.

With Spirit as the spearhead in our lives, we know that we do not need to be God but children of the Highest.

In Spirit, being a part of God is a source of great satisfaction and contentment.

After ego is tamed, ego is still available when necessary or needed, but not for use as "I" alone but as a humble assistant to the great "I AM" and a driving force for good.

When calling on ego insure that it is for Divine purpose and to glorify God. Ego, in this proper place will assist you in climbing the highest mountain and swimming the deepest sea with the right energy behind it.

And, ego can also be used to effectively fight and win battles also for the greater good.

However, remember it is foolish to underestimate ego, or deceive yourself about ego's basic, natural characteristics.

Never forget that if it walks like a duck, quacks like a duck, it is a duck.

Understand that in the layers of the egotistical mentality you will surely find a misguided, power seeking soul, which is capable of complete and utter destruction.

After you teach ego its rightful place in your life, you will find that ego becomes a grateful, joyful, student who eagerly submits and runs wanton no more although lays in wait for any opportunity.

1 Corinthians 1:25 - This foolish plan of God is wiser than the wisest of human plans, and God's weakness is stronger than the greatest of human strength.

And so, it is with Ego.

The Ego is not who you really are. The ego is your self-image; it is your social mask; it is the role you are playing.

Your social masks thrive on approval. It wants control, and it is sustained by power, because it lives in fear. ~ Deepak Chopra

## FEAR HAS NEVER CONQUERED ANYTHING!

## CHAPTER FIVE

# The Concept of Fear

Franklin D. Roosevelt during his first inaugural speech on March 4, 1933 stated:

*So, first of all, let me assert my firm belief that the only thing we have to fear is fear itself.*

President Roosevelt was talking about the economic conditions during the Great Depression, at the time he took office.

He was saying that the country needed to be more optimistic about the future of the economy, otherwise it would be hard to change anything.

He recognized the nature and power of fear to inhibit growth, development and more importantly, change the world.

Among many things which create change, fear has great power, negatively.

When we understand fear, it is clear that the danger of fear is in the power of beliefs and as a result the power it can manifest which has an ability stop or stifle positive action through perception.

Roosevelt went deeper into his definition regarding fear and defined it as, *nameless, unreasoning, unjustified terror which paralyzes needed efforts.*

The origins of fear can also be seen in the biblical account, again of Adam and Eve.

After the pair yielded to the deception of the serpent and ate the "Forbidden Fruit" from the "Tree of Knowledge of the Good and Evil," the Bible says that immediately,

"The eyes of both of them were opened, and they knew that they were naked."

This new awareness appeared to be more than just an awareness of physical nakedness. There appeared to be an immediate feeling of fear and a sense of foreboding.

Fear resulted in a sense of going against a higher plan, immediately, and as a result, fear became the nemesis of Divine Order as best it could.

In the bliss of a beautiful Garden of Eden, where there was only, love, light, joy, and adoration, the knowledge of fear reared its ugly head as a useful source of control.

Fear simply put is unawareness, fueled by a delusional perception of life, and a perceived, beforehand, negative outcome which is the nature of fear.

When both Adam and Eve realized they were exposed, they immediately felt guilt and shame for the first time in their lives. They also appeared terrified.

The biblical account then says, they then heard the sound of the Lord God walking in the Garden in the cool of the day, and Adam and his wife hid themselves from the presence of the Lord God among the trees of the garden. Then the Lord God called to Adam and said to him,

Where are you?

*Adam then said, I heard your voice in the garden, and I was afraid because I was naked; and I hid myself."*
(Genesis 3:8-10)

After eating the apple, seeking immediate elevation of consciousness, instead both were awakened into a very different reality immediately and at a very, very, basic level of understanding and removal from a higher frequency. Without the knowledge of fear there was nothing to fear because it did not exist in the human psyche and fear held no power or energy of thought.

Adam and Eve were exposed to new emotions and feelings which God, in wisdom, had not seen fit to give because fear is a lie. God as Creator already has full knowledge of everything, past, present and future, and it seems found fear a stumbling block to the Master's plan for humanity. However, the challenge then became the overcoming of fear as part of the new education.

It is interesting that Adam and Eve then made a covering from the leaves of a fig tree, the likely biblical fruit, later changed to a forbidden apple, by using the leaves from the tree of which eating caused the loss. Covering, in many forms can be seen as symbolic of hiding.

As a creation of God, we have two worlds within.

One world revolves around our appetites and the other revolves around an enlightened mind and Spirit. These two worlds are each always struggling for supremacy and dominance.

Many years later, Jesus the Christ cursed the fig tree, symbolizing the victory of the Christ Consciousness over the fall of the human soul which resulted in death and sin.

The Christ Consciousness is the growing human recognition and blending of the human evolutionary (or ego) mind with the *Divine Mind* and the *Divine Personality* that is the foundation for human happiness and fulfillment.

This awareness accrues over time within the consciousness of human thinking, when intention, attention and openness is focused on knowing in the "Christed" state of *being* and higher mindedness of enlightenment.

As this awareness in the human mind grows and strengthens, life becomes more liberated, joyful, peaceful, and love oriented.

The fear which creates isolation and despair begins to diminish in thought and feeling. You are free to live the life you were born to live as a child of Spirit in a love-filled and supportive universe.

This is what it is all about I believe.

It is also interesting to note that God then made a coat of skins as a more appropriate covering considering their condition, which interestingly required the first sacrifice of a living being to obtain the covering.

This again is connected to the Christ Consciousness and a later sacrifice by crucifixion of Jesus the Christ and related also to Old Testament animal sacrifices which pointed to a greater and eternal sacrifice which would bring the soul of humanity back to the path and return to the Edenic state.

While some teachings in structured religions teach the physical coming of a man in the sky for the Second Coming, in reality, the universal Christ Consciousness, within our hearts and minds, as a powerful awakening, is the apocalypse meaning unveiling, and some would argue the Second Coming.

Perhaps the greatest and most powerful element of fear itself, after the fall, was the revelation of death as stated. The dynamic of death brought a type of desperation, due to the perception of the human soul as no longer immortal, limited, and a feeling originated of every man for himself.

Initially, the Earth, it appears, was said to be designed as a place for God's other creations.

Before man's arrival, other species, such as dinosaurs, for example, roamed the Earth for thousands of years.

Genesis 1:24-26 states that humans were created after animals and that, in fact, the first man and woman were created simultaneously.

1:24 - And God said, let the earth bring forth the living creature after his kind, cattle, and creeping thing, and beast of the earth after his kind: and it was so.

1:25 - And God made the beast of the earth after his kind and cattle after their kind, and everything that creepeth upon the earth after his kind: and God saw that it was good.

1:26 - And God said, let us make man in our image, after our likeness: and let them have dominion over the fish of the sea, and over the fowl of the air, and over the cattle, and over all the earth, and over every creeping thing that creepeth upon the earth.

After eating the fruit, Adam and Eve also became aware of animal instincts and sexual urges defined, as id or libido explained earlier, as a dynamic and definite characteristic of personal satisfaction. This, again, is revealed by their attempt to instantly cover their naked bodies.

More poignant than any revelation in the story of the so-called fall of man is the revelation of the feeling of fear's capability as a crippling mental prison.

On our journey through this 3D or Third *Dimension* it is one of the most powerful mechanisms used which can deny fulfillment of the dreams and purpose, individually, and collectively in the world.

Sadly, many die regretful of not accomplishing some type of goal due to fear. And more importantly, many wars are started after the perception and manipulation by fear at the foundation.

Today, as we come down the home stretch, more so than in any time in the history of human life, we can and are being manipulated and controlled through various forces which subtly promote a fearful existence, for example, again, through the media and even by various highly advanced little known, technologies designed for bioelectric influence of the human and body.

In the ever-present attempt to mimic Divine presence, our buddy Ego continues to try to replicate life, and what God created in many, many ways and forms.

A good example is scientific cloning and the Transhuman agenda seeking to create a half human and half robot species and much more.

Some would argue that those that were created by the Adversary, or having willing accepted the *Mark of the Beast* of the Adversary, capturing their minds, do so at the cost of denial of the immortal soul and as a result seek others ways, to resist casting into the "Lake of Fire."

Today everything that God created is being strategically destroyed from not only the human psyche, to all life in general, plants, vegetation, food - genetically modified, animals, bees, fluoride in water, manipulation of the climate, and the contamination of the ocean through radiation leakage and oil spill. However, through great turmoil the earth has survived for eons.

The fact is, the illusion of fear and doubt cowardly disappears when truth arrives on the scene.

With the understanding of God's perfect and ultimate good by plan, we become free from fear. We learn to trust and take chances and understand that death, while in the Spirit of God, from this plane is purely physical, and a passing or homecoming to existence.

We were never cut off, we were just on vacation, in the drama of this life. The whole world is literally the stage.

We are in a precarious time in the history of man and woman at this juncture on this planet.

We are on a path designated and prepared for a leap into a new Age of Enlightenment.

Fear, which has played a pivotal role, through entrapment, in the grand scheme is now dissipating and revealed for what is truly is – nothing and lacking real power.

Fear not, because God is surely with us, always has been, and always will be, no matter what the false appearance or any circumstances.

*For God hath not given us a spirit of fear; but of power, and of love, and of a sound mind.*

--2 Timothy 1:7

A sound mind is the key word here. Do not be deceived.

**CHAPTER SIX**

# The Concept of Oneness

*One drop of water taken from the ocean is just as perfect ocean water as the whole great body.*

*The constituent elements of water are exactly the same, and they are combined in precisely the same ratio or perfect relation to each other, whether we consider one drop, a pail full, a barrelful, or the entire ocean out of which the lesser quantities are taken; each is complete in itself; they differ only in quantity or degree.*

*Each contains the whole, and yet no one would make the mistake of supposing from this statement that each drop is the entire ocean.*

*So, we say that each individual manifestation of God contains the whole; not for a moment meaning that each is God in His entirety, so to speak, but that each is God come forth, shall I say, in different quantity or degrees.*

The Heart is another Name for God

*Excerpt,* "Lessons in Truth" ~ H. Emily Cady.

And so, it is with humanity. A bucket taken from a bucket is still a bucket.

An acorn has within itself the ability to grow to perfection as an Oak tree. However, the tree is influenced by the circumstances of the soil, the climate, and environmental conditions. However, the energy assisting growth never changes.

The message:

*We are one in the same Spirit as evolving, lesser degrees, of God.*

In the book, *Codependence: The Dance of Wounded Soul* the author,

Robert Burney writes:

*We all have available to us - within - a direct channel to the Highest Vibrational Frequency Range within the illusion. That highest range involves consciousness of the Glory of Oneness. It is called Cosmic Consciousness. It is called Christ Consciousness. However, the progressive consciousness is called many names by many traditions, throughout history.*

*It has been called Enlightenment, Self-Realization, Nirvana, or Cosmic Consciousness. These various terms appear to be defining the connection of self to real self through the personality self into light and bliss and Divine Reality. The location within where all things are known is*

*experienced. It results in knowledge of only good no matter what the educational experiences on the material plane.*

I must first clarify my perception that the concept of *Oneness* is not connected to the egotistical ideation of the so called "New World Order or more precisely "Disorder" being promoted through a decisive globalization agenda it appears. This goal is today blatantly revealed in our faces as a decisive Luciferian agenda.

As described, *Oneness* is a part of the whole originating from the whole.

The oneness of which I speak is the decisive awareness that humanity as a whole is the creation of One God, in One Love unified.

With caution, and to avoid any typical egotistical misunderstanding, I say we are in a sense little Gods on Earth by likeness.

The key word is "little" that we must never forget which Satan did.

In Christ Consciousness, we know that every woman or man is our father and mother, brother or sister and that everything and everyone emanated from God.

However, as discussed, much of our true selves becomes lost in the translation of the unconscious mind. This again, is through our senses, in this reality which leaves us with a feeling of separation from the whole due, by false reporting of five sense perceptions.

Those that are promulgating the globalization agenda, it appears, without a doubt recognize the powerful potential of mass programmed "thought control" to assist in the manifestation of the effort because of the capability of thought to become tangible reality.

The so-called Illuminati also know that because of the factual oneness of all life, that an idea can be implanted, manifested in one person and with great power flow throughout all of humanity, gradually, eventually, becoming reality because of our connection to each other. Creating reality becomes a highly effective method for control and dominance.

Because of this power, *Oneness* must be clarified.

If misunderstood, the dynamic of oneness could be used to assist in the New World, global effort or more accurately, again, The New World Disorder agenda by use of the power of the human mind again, the ability of creative thought. This is the powerful creative force necessary for the New World Disorder agenda to factually materialize.

For example, a powerful figure, working towards this agenda, is on the record saying that the goal is being slowed by the connection of humanity globally by the internet.

This is because of information regarding the effort is being passed within humanity and a consciousness is created which is against the thought or the ideal.

For this reason, Oneness as a Spiritual Concept of unification and connection and not as a superficial concept, rendering a complete understanding of use as a powerful tool is pivotal.

The *Oneness* of which I speak is awareness of the spiritual unification and alignment with the Source of all Good which acknowledges, as mentioned earlier, consciously, the connection to everything and everyone meaning only good and without bloodshed.

We experience this connection, for example, on a smaller scale with those in our environment and those who we love.

Also, as mentioned, in the physical, material realm humanity views itself as separate from others and even separated from God as untruth.

In reality, all of God's creation has the same life force within. The spiritual realm, where the super Conscious resides, is fully aware of the human connection to all life is uncontested and absolute.

Our connection manifests in many ways.

For example, when pulling into the parking garage to start my day at work years ago, distracted, I accidentally cut another vehicle off.

Irate, the driver yelled at me, with such intensity that my good mood changed. Subconsciously, as I exited my vehicle, and entered my place of employment, I then snapped at someone else.

In the connection of oneness, what was passed on to me was then passed on to someone else and likely so on and so on. Oneness involves not only the ability to pass on positivity but also the ability to pass on negativity as well.

An excerpt from the website "Spirit of Oneness" defines oneness by first asking:

What does "Spirit of Oneness mean?"

It means:

*We live in a world where individualism is encouraged to the extent where we sometimes consider ourselves separate from one another. But we are all inextricably linked in so many ways – physically, emotionally, mentally and spiritually.*

The author further states:

*We believe that we come from One Source to which we will all return and, even though we appear to be separate during our physical existence on Mother Earth, we are, in truth, all one.*

*Life is a series of challenges, all at different levels, and we can more easily meet these in a state of inspired and creative thought, with joy, peace, serenity, if we learn to accept and love our connection with all other souls.*

It does not get any clearer than this.

Oneness is the reality that we ultimately affect others through an unbroken chain spearheaded by our divine connection.

Perhaps the greatest Metaphysician of all, Jesus the Christ, knew of, used, and understood this concept when he so eloquently declared "My Father and I Are One."

Some would argue that he was saying that he is God and other say not so. Some would argue that what he really meant is that God and *ALL* of God's creation are one with God.

The acknowledgement of "Not my will but God's will be done" is another example of asking, through trust, the will of the indwelling God, to take over the direction of our lives.

This simple request not only ignites the recognition and acknowledgement of the God within, and our oneness with God, by asks God to glorify God's Spirit, above all else. It also is a form of the highest of praise.

Metaphysics is the systematic study of the Science of Being. It studies that which transcends the physical.

Christ: The "anointed one." The God-self of each person is our divine potential and true identity.

In specific metaphysical terms – it is the perfect idea of being in the "Mind of God."

Christ's acceptance and awareness of oneness with God enabled the manifestation of great miracles on his path on Earth. And, so it is with all.

The closeness to God, known by Jesus, was through his awareness of the never-broken chain which allowed him to willingly walked his path, fearlessly, and suffer, for the good of God, on this plane, knowing in advance that he would return home to "Our Father/Mother God."

This energy was on a mission. This realization was so powerful that his awareness of being one with God, would later serve to enlighten souls for thousands of years to come because of the absolute truth of the connection.

To activate this power, the consciousness needed only to humbly acknowledge that God is the great "I AM," and this spirit a follower of the great "I AM" and there is nothing else.

The awareness of Oneness then activated the real authentic power prevalent in God's Universe electromagnetically and a higher frequency and begin drawing energy to his Divine purpose.

As discussed previously, it is through consciousness, that we first recognize that we exist and through the consciousness awakening we can begin to change and right the wrongs of this world together.

It is no secret that good intent creates and attracts alignment with good and vice versa.

Good intent is a result of being assured of something as factual beforehand confidently.

Truth has no duality and is absolute and final.

Although, again, we simply must have dual experiences in life to get to the gift of absolute truth I believe. By comparison there is no other way.

In other words, there is always, good and evil, negative and positive, love and hate, man and woman, yes and no, etc., duality.

Through Oneness and alignment with God and God's good intentions, we affect our environment and the world and activate the power available for good use which reigns supreme in the Universe.

There is great strength and power in the alignment when there is acknowledgement of its reality.

This truth can create a powerful group consciousness and set us free from the nagging discontentment that something is out of sync or out of place defined by our misconceptions, five sense intellect and beliefs.

With this understanding in our hearts and minds at this moment, stop and imagine where this world will be if all hope for the very best and make the decision to see and create love, understanding, and embrace, forgive one another recognizing we are the mirror images of each other in varying degrees. It is just that easy to create by the power of unified thought.

Can you see it? Many can.

We are comprised of everything which God is.

When a soul enters the material plane, the material plane then becomes the foundation for learning and hope to return back to Eden state.

Where could our world and planet be if the first thing we are taught at the beginning of our advent that we are not here solely for the purpose of acquiring material possessions, which rust and decay, but instead to be a presence for the betterment on the planet and advance good above all else, the real reason, first, far most and above all other efforts.

This is the real hidden treasure and something which lingers in our souls forever and of which never decays and transitions with us?

Would not the results of life on this planet be completely different from the world in which we see and live now in the Matrix?

The key, *Seek the kingdom of God first and all things will surely be given onto us.*

As we evolve into a higher spiritual vibration, the Christ Consciousness, the indwelling Spirit of God, begins to express itself as we move forward.

All life evolves.

It is inevitable that the "*All Good*" presence, a derivative of the "*ALL God*," dynamic ultimately will have its way.

The Christ Consciousness or understanding which Jesus knew profoundly continues to materialize by perfectly timed revelations.

Little known is that, all of the law-givers chosen by God have been *Iesu* and are known by these terms: I-es-u, of which Yeshuah the actual name of Jesus is derived.

When the Constantine Bible was written by the Nicene Creed in the fourth century, the word Jesus was used as symbolism.

Capilya of India, Ka'yu or Confucius of China, Po of China, Zarathustra of Persia, Chine of China, Joshu of Israel were all naturally born Iesus.

In some religions, it is believed that the human soul can attain *Iesu* status by fasting, long suffering and diet. Brahma, for example, attained Iesu status in his old age.

Iesu, signifying, without evil, is the ultimate salvation of the soul and that which the soul longs for in its longing for ascension and the homecoming is the return to the Garden.

When we become without evil, after recognizing it clearly, the soul attains and becomes one with the *All* Light, and is then, Iesu.

The Spirit of God is both masculine and feminine.

In Christian mysticism, the concept of Sophia balances the Christ Consciousness as the dual sexless nature of Iesu.

In Latin Sophia is co-existent with the Trinity, operating as the feminine aspect of God. This energy, Philo-Sophia, is the "Wisdom of God" which throughout the ages wills only the good that binds us.

Philo means that one expresses love in a world that is fixed and Sophy is Latin for knowledge. It is translated into "Love of Wisdom."

The balance created by two opposing, powerful forces, ultimately must unite the feminine and masculine energy long out of sync through Ego driven negative aggression, one sided teaching, and will produce a profound spiritual shift, and healing.

This is the nature of balance.

It is no mistake that masculine energy has been pushed forward and feminine energy intentionally diminished by the energy of "You know who." When energy is misplaced or one sided, it results in chaos in life.

The result is a deviant abundance of energy which does not have an equal force necessary for balance and as a result creates dysfunction and energy is out of sync.

The *Wisdom of God* is defined in the New Testament when Jesus directly mentions Wisdom in the Gospel of Matthews:

> The Son of man came eating and drinking, and they say, Behold a man gluttonous, and a winebibber, a friend of publicans and sinners. But wisdom is justified of her children...
>
> — Matthew 11:19

St. Paul refers to the concept, notably in, 1 Corinthians, but obscurely, deconstructing worldly wisdom:

> Where is the wise? Where is the scribe? Where is the disputer of this world? Hath not God made foolish the wisdom of this world?
>
> —1 Corinthians 1:20.

Paul sets worldly wisdom against a higher wisdom of God:

> But we speak the wisdom of God in a mystery, even the hidden wisdom, which God ordained before the world unto our glory.
>
> —1 Corinthians 2:7

The Epistle of James (James 3:13-18; cf. James 1:5) distinguishes between two kinds of wisdom. One is a false wisdom, which is characterized as:

> "earthly, sensual, and devilish" and is associated with strife and contention.

The other is the 'wisdom that comes from above':

> But the wisdom that is from above is first pure, then peaceable, gentle, [and] easy to be in treated, full of mercy and good fruits, without partiality, and without hypocrisy.
>
> —James 3:17

As humanity moves forward, the deficient Sophia energetic influence derived from *perfect wisdom* is thrusting itself forward seeking to rectify the long-endured imbalance by reconnecting the missing link.

God's polar wisdom of balance is essentially claiming its rightful place in our hearts and minds as we awaken.

It is doing so out of the chaos manifested by the patriarchal, masculine energy running wanton due to the lack of the balancing effect of the powerful feminine energy principle.

Masculine energy has governed by egotistical dominance because of the denial of our beloved Creator as masculine and feminine energy or as a sexless force, and only a male energy as a whole.

It simply is not true and is in reality another characteristic of the failed doctrines and false teachings of some structured religions. The fact is God is not a person.

In one publication dating back to the late 1800s, Jehovih (father) and Om (mother) are the two names of the Creator as one. Other references are "The Great

Spirit", "The All Person", the unseen and ever-present. God is also a title for once mortal or in corporeal form (spirit within a body).

The Creator is all and was all and forever will be all. The Creator is our father and mother, and all that are and were born are our family. We are one. With this knowledge, we access to the Christ Consciousness energy within just as surely as Jesus the Christ.

As we began to consciously lift ourselves out of the vibration of this diminishing pervading lower electromagnetic energy field, in timed ascension, we start the evolution through choosing to work and live together in harmony.

As a result, we have begun the Second Coming of the message of Universal love.

There is no place within our Hearts and hopefully true also for those empowered by evil for evil and ruthless evil acts.

There will be some resistance to this energy, however, the struggle within inevitably will dissipate and the Christ Consciousness will assuredly have its way.

Although we cannot remember the contractual agreement, on our path to both involution and evolution, we no longer see separation and in full awareness of *Oneness* move forward together into the glorious Light of recognition and released.

Acknowledging this, and making it our reality, changes everything in our lives, the lives of others, and the world around us and a renewed path on the journey home.

Oneness affords forgiveness which is the natural outcome of love and understanding at a higher level of consciousness.

On the higher level the spiritual intention, for good, begins to right delusions and illusions, and begins to affect and change lives, and influence the world globally.

We then become the change we want to see beginning with ourselves.

A seed, the size of a mustard seed is planted, and it results in phenomenal growth.

As the chaos and misconception of our true purpose is redirected into light, the evolutionary process demands that we naturally, in our individual spiritual growth, and collective spiritual advancement, access a new vibrational frequency on the road to awakening ultimately leading to the eight sense.

The journey has given illumination, reconnecting each of us to our infinite soul. In this state of being, we recognize that all that had defined our world as separation has been an unreal. The Puppet Master loses.

There is an abrupt change, a sudden increase in knowledge, and a powerful surge of conscious awakening together.

As we unfold in this vibration, and embrace this inner glow of recognition within our hearts, we truly become that which we are, and always have been, part of the magnificent, unified whole.

We connect with *all* life and take the quantum leap..

*Neither shall they say, lo here! Or, lo there! For, behold, the kingdom of god is within you.*

- Luke 17:21

**"WE ALSO ARE OUR BROTHER'S KEEPER!"**

**CHAPTER SEVEN**

# Fifth Dimension Consciousness

The transformation from third dimensional consciousness to the next has begun in various steps.

As we cross into the fifth dimension, passing through the fourth, we awaken in the fifth dimension where Co-creation with our beloved God begins.

*The frequencies of the first three dimensions interact together and are collectively called by Man the Physical or Material Plane, or called the "Third Dimension" for simplicity.*

*Man does not recognize the presence of the first and second dimensions, though the expressions of both are in constant evidence all around them as the framework and fabric of their everyday existence.*

*The third in which we live now and the fourth dimensions are comprised of Matter Substance, the lowest frequencies of Substance in Creation.*

*Under normal conditions and circumstances, reportedly, the higher consciousness does not exist in either the fourth or third dimensions.*

*Such populations live temporarily within the fourth and third dimensions are said to live within a time line.*

*Populations living within a time line lead very illusionary existences which non-the-less seem very real to them.*

Excerpt from *The Seven Dimensions of the Outer Creation,* Cliff R. Livingstone.

While this human transformation is common knowledge in certain esoteric circles, because of studies of ancient knowledge and philosophy, many of humanity are unaware of the progression taking place literally right before our eyes.

"Out of Chaos Comes Order."

In this case, "Order" is not the Globalist concept and hope for global control as they think. There is a greater power involved little do they know.

Instead "Divine Order" will evolve founded on the highest principles and the highest frequency of love and not that which is founded on the evil, delusions, or psychopathic power of dwindling control by those motivating New World Order fueled by bloodshed and representatives of Satan.

I remember a musical group called the Fifth Dimension. Of the songs, they are remembered for is one of which the lyrics reveal, *This is the Dawning of the Age of Aquarius* and hope for universal global peace and brotherly love to come. On a metaphysical level, many have always been aware of the continued evolution of humanity.

As December 21, 2012 neared, most did not know what to expect. Many waited in suspense for a catastrophe negatively.

The fact that the Mayan calendar placed significance on this year as having special meaning further perplexed many as this date came and went without any obvious sensation.

Could the Mayan calendar, stopping in 2012, actually mean the ending of one-dimensional level of consciousness, and the advancement, and birthing into the next dimension many asked?

What if the Mayan's knew that the shift of consciousness was inevitable, a phenomenon having been charted for eons, and thereby believed it unnecessary to define the progression as the old inevitably passes away?

Or, perhaps the Mayans knew that 2012 would bring a new path and begin the next evolutionary phase of expansion?

Carl Johan, author of "The Mayan Calendar and Transformation of Consciousness" writes:

*The prophetic Mayan Calendar is not keyed to the movements of planetary bodies. Instead, it functions as a metaphysical map of the evolution of conscious-ness and records how spiritual time flows, providing a new science of time.*

The dimensions are defined as:

1. First dimension is Intelligence or conscious awareness. Humanities first dimensional consciousness is 'unconscious' to our five physical senses. It is the illusion of separation. We understand we exist but have no clue why. It is our first awakening to a physical presence without, the first necessary experiences which teaches us. It is the journey outwards and away from the One. Because there is also a tendency to wobble or distort as the intense learning, exploration process begins, we can easily forget our true nature. Because of the vulnerability, an illusion called fear enters, and we begin to imagine or believe that there are others who are "different" from us, and that to protect your group you must repel these others. You imagine that their differences threaten you, and so you seek to eliminate them to create "sameness" again. And so,

the illusion produces negative vibrations called fear, hatred, aggression and war.

2. Second dimension is Energy diminished by Intelligence and Substance. The consciousness of this dimension does not possess self-awareness but relies on the awakening five senses. Second dimensional consciousness is only aware of the need for feeding, fighting, and procreation. Second dimensional consciousness lives solely within the moment and in the "Survival of the Fittest" mode. This is also the point where consciousness discovers its own personal inherent creative power, and knowledge of the creativity formed by union with another that there can be a productive manifestation and creation of life.

   The intense creative power of the expression of love is equally matched by the destructive nature of the fear illusion at this level also. If the consciousness falls into the illusion of being separate and alone, its interpretation of survival might mean it has to use or manipulate the intense energies at this level to eliminate others who threaten its needs being met. Getting further away from the Universal Light Force, it has forgotten the One.

3. Third dimension is Substance diminished by Intelligence and Energy. In the third dimension, life takes shape and mirrors all that we are seeking to learn and understand by revelation through experience. In third dimensional consciousness is the

school room that has been set into place to learn and understand creation. Third dimensional collective awareness, in itself, seeks to prove that there is no other reality than what we perceive by our limited five senses because the senses report that no other consciousness exists. It understands the principle of the One as related to humans, who are seen as the highest level of intelligence, since they have left the second level and "raised" to the third.

When one is fully in the Consciousness of the One, then you are truly aware that the concept of hierarchy is a third dimensional construct that has been created in ignorance and out of the nature of the One.

In its true vibration of resonance with the One, the third dimension is a place where humans can create structures to flow their energies and assist them to manifest whatever they wish in the plane of matter.

However, when consciousness moves into the direction of fear at this level, it becomes suspicious of the motives and thoughts of others who are different. It then begins to set up structures that will control and manage thought and energy, to the benefit of those who manage the structures. As a result, in 3D is the rise of institutions such as churches, universities, hospitals, schools, and banks and charitable organizations. All set up within the philanthropic motivation of the third density desire to structure, but when subjected to fear it distorts and become instruments for control and personal enrichment for a few at the expense of many.

4. Fourth dimension is Expansion. Its dimensional attribution is Substance/Energy where Intelligence is the diminished factor. On the fourth dimension, we can reconnect to the group identity without loss of self and recognize existence as part of a whole. In the fourth dimension, thought and feeling create reality, much more quickly than on the third dimension. Fear can create evil as surely as love can create happiness, joy, and beauty.

The Law of One states that we are all One. We derive from the source that we are all interconnected. Through Cause and Effect, we understand that what we do affects all life and the equilibrium and vice versa. This is the reason for the teachings of the Christ of "do unto others as you would have them do unto you."

Fear has attempted it egotistical control also, however, at this level the consciousness we begin to understand fully that fear is an illusion that denies Oneness and that fear is a byproduct of separation and that it perpetuates feelings of isolation and loneliness. At this level, we can know and begin to experience the concept of "family" and in *Divine Oneness*. We understand that we are all related and in relationship, no matter who, or where, we are in place or time.

We must learn to view all human relationships from this higher consciousness.

5. Fifth dimension, of which we head, is the bottom line of Creation. It is the dimension where Ascendancy begins the evolution of the human soul and under normal circumstance descendancy works at the lower light. Essentially the journey home has begun. The character of the fifth dimension is perfection. Its dimensional attribution is Intelligence/Substance where Energy is the diminished factor. Fifth dimension lives in the unified reality of consciousness of Spirit. All actions on the fifth dimension are based on love which is the only absolute reality.

   At this point the consciousness, having begun to re-awaken to the mysteries of creation, desires to gain wisdom and experience of the Creator. The consciousness seeks to fully experience itself as a Co-Creator of its own holographic reality in partnership with the Divine.

6. Sixth Dimensional consciousness is Oneness with the "Spark of God or Deity" within all life in its rightful place. The characteristic of the sixth dimension is creativity. Its dimensional attribution is Intelligence / Energy. Substance is the diminished factor.

7. Seventh Dimensional consciousness is the awakening to full awareness of the real mission and purpose of life. The seventh dimension activates a desire to make a difference in the world. At the seventh level

of consciousness you identify with your physical environment and start living from your heart, mind, spirit and soul daily in tune with the Universal Light Force and enlightened.

8. At the Eighth level of consciousness you identify with your environment and with others and have full control over the story of life and your existence on Earth. We began to create the good and the world we want to see.

9. At the Ninth level of consciousness you identify with full cosmic consciousness. You endeavor to become responsible for stewardship on the planet. Stewardship is the theological belief that humans are responsible for the world around us, and all existence, and that we should take care and nurture all life. You become pure energy within and you can transform others through powerful magnetic healing energy.

10. At the Tenth level the golden ray of Universal Consciousness is inaugurated into being as a full expression of the Universal Light Force. The universal level of consciousness is achieved. You have returned home, are now One, and aligned in Unity of Consciousness with the physical form of your Local Universe.

Today, as progression continues some within humanity are awakening in the fifth dimension of consciousness.

Within this Heart centered awakening is destined *Divine Unity*.

The fifth dimension is the beginning step of the return to the metaphysical, symbolic Garden of Eden of which we left to gain knowledge intentionally.

In astrology, Aquarius ruled by Uranus is the sign of expansion and brotherly love. While the crossover from one Age to the next can take hundreds of years, the critical midpoint between the Age of Pisces and the Age of Aquarius was December 21st, 2012 AD, when the Earth's equatorial plane aligned exactly with the galactic center. The Age of Aquarius (2012 to 4142) is said will usher in a period of unity, love, peace, along with a greater understanding of the purpose of humanity and an expanded, brought by Uranus, the planet of expansion, understanding of the Universe and our connection to it.

Each astrological sign is attached to a planet and said to be influenced by the energy emitted by the planet which sends out powerful rays as exampled by the energy Earth experiences and receives from the Moon.

The doctrine of the Age of Aquarius, if compared with the biblical "New Earth" and elevated consciousness, said to manifest during this time period should bring global consciousness ascension.

Each Age has a theme, and the theme of the Age of Pisces was Christianity (Sagittarius is on the Mid-heaven). Both Pisces and Sagittarius are "spiritual" signs interested in the larger meaning of life. The theme(s) of the coming Age of Aquarius will be truth and brotherhood.

This change to the Aquarian age is so important because it changes the astrological conditions for the entire planet. Every person on planet Earth has been and will be affected by this shift. The Piscean Age had also been dominated by hierarchy, and power which now begins to diminish.

Astrology essentially is a man-made science based on the subconscious instinctual reality of man's intuitive observations. Ancient civilizations first observed and charted the constellations by connecting the dots of stars in the sky creating images of a ram, bull, twins, etc.

It was by observation and instinct that man observed that, during certain times of the month, August for example, that the personality a person born during certain times behaved in a certain manner and exhibited characteristics attributed to that of a lion for example.

## The Age of Aquarius defined:

Ages are believed by some astrologers to affect mankind while other astrologers believe the Ages correlate to the rise and fall of mighty civilizations and cultural tendencies. Aquarius traditionally "rules" electricity, computers, and flight, to include, democracy, freedom, humanitarianism, idealists, modernization, astrology, nervous disorders, rebels and rebellion.

Other keywords and ideas believed associated with Aquarius are nonconformity, philanthropy, veracity, perseverance, humanity and irresolution. The appearance or elevation in status of many of these Aquarian developments over the last few centuries is considered by many astrologers to indicate the proximity of the Aquarian age.

There is no uniform agreement about the relationship of these recent Aquarian developments and the Age of Aquarius.

Some believe that the influence of a New Age is experienced before it arrives because of a Cuspal effect or Orb of Influence. Others believe the appearance of Aquarian developments; indicate the actual arrival of the Age of Aquarius.

In order to understand the age of Aquarius, we must first understand the influence of the planet Uranus which rules the sign and the energy it emits. Uranus, among all planets, most governs genius.

Historically, it was associated with the principles of enlightenment and radical political ideas of equality and freedom, among other things. Around the period of its discovery in 1781, the idea of democracy was prevalent, with the breakaway of the American colonies from England and a few years later in 1789, the French revolution.

Rest assured, do not dismay. We are in the transformation.

*"life is a balance between transformation and resistance to transformation. Think of yourself as a dancer on the blurry edge separating order from chaos."*

~ Fred Alan Wolf, Ph.D.

# CHAPTER EIGHT

# Global Change

I do believe that the Moon does affect human emotions and earth changes as a powerful influential body.

Because of this I found the belief of the destruction of outdated power structures, no longer effective or in sync with a new beginning for Mother Earth and its inhabitants an interesting concept.

Mundane astrology is the application of astrology to world affairs and world events, taking its name from the Latin word Mundus, meaning "the World." Mundane astrology is a branch of judicial astrology and is widely believed by astrological historians to be the most ancient branch.

In the middle Ages, mundane astrology was more commonly known as the study of Revolutions - meaning the study of the revolutions of the planets in their apparent orbits around the Earth, as they were then believed to do.

Political astrology is a branch of mundane astrology dealing with politics, the government, politicians and laws governing a particular nation, state, or city. A wider definition of mundane astrology focuses also on natural and man-made disasters.

On January 24, 2008, Pluto entered Capricorn until June 13, 2008 and then its re-entered Capricorn on November 26, 2008 and will remain until November 20, 2024. We are currently living under the influence of Pluto in Capricorn which demands, restructure of government and the world globally, until 2024, as government structures began to crumble it is said.

Pluto in Capricorn means transformation of the foundation of structures, such as government, religion, and ineffective educational systems for example. As the universal transformation comes into play:

*Don't ask yourself what the world needs; ask yourself what makes you come alive. And then go and do that. Because what the world needs are people who have come alive.*

– Howard Thurman

Sheeple no more.

Pluto changing signs into Capricorn is a rare and significant event with far-reaching global effects. Since Pluto is, indeed, the "Great Transformer" its purpose is upheaval, reform and regeneration and it is destined to transform whatever it is impacting. It will bring this overhaul type energy to those areas Capricorn rules, which are:

- The economy, corporations, banking and big business.

- Government and its policy influence and actions at all levels (local, national and global).

- Politics and political activities (i.e. elections, voting issues, law, etc.).

- Societal laws, rules and regulations.

- Churches and organized religion, and the dogmas and rituals they adhere to.

- The patriarchal system in general.

These are all areas that need extreme change and transformation, and it is happening as protests all over the world against these structures, which are now revealed as self-serving, manipulative, ineffective, outdated and useless to humanity's global new position. Pluto in Capricorn's influence is destined to bring about events and massive changes overall.

Many systems and entities will go through Plutonic-like transformations. These institutions will be held to greater accountability, as many injustices and wrong doings will come to the light under the piercing eye of the accuracy of the plutonian dissection. Agencies and organizations that have been trying to keep various aspects of their dealings and intentions "hidden" or away from public view and scrutiny will find themselves in the midst of a scandal or investigation, and shadow government revealed.

Agencies that are especially in need of transforming, yet resist, may also crumble or even cease to exist altogether under the pressures of the Age of Aquarius and Pluto in Capricorn. The sign of Capricorn also rules karma and the results of past actions. Nothing goes unaccounted for and the next few years, as defined by astrologist, are surely to be a time of atonement for past actions.

The synonym for Capricorn is purpose or purposeful. The energy emitted by the sign, always has purpose and is willing to try and reach its goal, using all possible means. Capricorn sweeps away everything, absolutely, and works precisely, definitely, and rigidly, while advancing towards its target, in this case outdated power structures. The altruistic goal of the Capricorn Saturn is always working for, devoted to, and for the benefit for others.

We have already seen some of the power that Pluto has in the recent financial crisis. It appears that a lot more is to come. Misuse of power is an area that Pluto is especially adept and likely to investigate. But typical of the profound *Wisdom of God*, these things will happen in their own way and in its own time and we must accept the changes as part of the design and grand scheme.

Pluto, it is said, has work to do, and it will have plenty of time to do it. It will be in this position for the next 15 years, bringing lasting change. However, as is the nature of profound change, it always requires first destruction, turmoil, and chaos before transformation is realized. But it will be worth it for generations to come.

Pluto is here to make things right. Pluto the mythological god of the underworld has a way of working at such deep levels that sometimes when manifests goes unseen to the conscious level until it appears in reality. Pluto will create powerful change, and in record time.

As the demise of government control etches its way into the world and transforms everyone, and everything, at the conscious awakening level, there are those who have been holding the reins and who will vainly seek to resist or even prevent what is on the horizon, as previously mentioned through the globalized ideation for this planet.

The foundation for their efforts is to remain in power and thwart the awakening by any means possible, and to continue to promote and deny awareness of humanity as factually having power to Co-Create good and the ability to heal and renew the Earth and all life. For humanity and the world, however, the transformation is universally ordained and inevitable and of such great propensity that it cannot be stopped by any arrogant, deviant energy.

Be assured that we are in the inevitable awakening and the resulting powerful unified unification energy of spiritual wholeness, through with each other and the Creator resulting in the expression and expansion of real authentic power which is lovingly, quietly, ruling, guiding, directing and transforming.

The effects of the Pluto in Capricorn planetary positioning can already be seen as exposure of hidden agendas by a small group, or the 1%, comprised of Elitist: bankers, corporations, secret societies, government officials, and other dominant and intentionally, disguised and hidden, groups such as the Bilderberg Group, Council of Foreign Relations and the Trilateral Commission and secret societies.

The Globalist agenda whose sole desire, reportedly, it appears is to remain in power, continue to control humanity, and direct all life on this planet, want to play God. And through research, testing and development of highly advanced, globally placed, electromagnetic technology, documented as capable of powerfully deploying extremely low frequency for global manipulation and influence, the Adversary's toys and minions are in place in hope of thwarting Divine Order.

The globalization effort includes the use of literally thousands of satellites orbiting Earth. It includes Drones, and some believe research at the High Frequency Active Auroral Project or HAARP facility, scientific methods for weather manipulation, the Ground Wave Energy Network or GWEN and microwave cellular towers combined as a weapon system, and even hologram technology which can, and has been used to project an image of religious terror, using common religious belief taught to the masses by structured religion as a control mechanism.

Effectiveness may be the result of humanity's longing for change and hope for, as some religions believe, a Christ figure to literally return in the sky and rescue us all. This technology is no joke, and is officially patented, at the United States Patent and Trademark Office revealing it as very real and along with hundreds of similar consciousness altering patents.

The technology is capable of powerful deception in the unaware through electromagnetic, electronic manipulation and influence, of not only individuals, or small groups, but also large populations, simultaneously, and it is patented as capable of creating a delusional and false reality through effects which includes perception management through tampering with and manipulation of brainwaves through this global system and a super computer, brain interface system.

We must stay alert and aware of the advancement of brilliant, mind control, psychophysical patented technologies, invented for mass, social population control and to stop the awakening. The technology and its use are detailed in my "Mind Control Technology Amazon six book series.

Many believe this technology can be attributed to biblical text referring to the Adversary's materialization of technology so powerful that is has the manifestation capabilities of producing a delusional "Voice of God" effect although man-made. And in the Military Industrial Complex, it is factually known as such:

2 Thessalonians speaks of technology capable of manifesting strong delusions during this critical time of transformation. And today, thousands, report globally, their personal experiences and the effectiveness of this highly advanced, and, again, patented, electromagnetic technology capable of global mind control electronically:

*And then the lawless one will be revealed whom the Lord will consume with the breath of His mouth and destroy with the brightness of His coming.*

The coming of the lawless one. This is according to the working of Satan, with all power, signs, and lying wonders, and with all unrighteous deception among those who perish, because they did not receive the love of the truth, that they might be saved.

And for this reason, God will send them strong delusion that they should believe the lie that they all may be condemned who did not believe the truth but had pleasure in unrighteousness.

But we are bound to give thanks to God always for you, brethren beloved by the Lord, because God from the beginning chose you for salvation through sanctification by the Spirit and belief in the truth, to which He called you by our gospel, for the obtaining of the glory of our Lord Jesus Christ.

*Therefore, brethren, stand fast and hold the traditions which you were taught, whether by word or our epistle.*

--- 2 Thessalonians 2:8-15.

This technology was factually used in the Iraqi War, as the voice of Allah, beamed electromagnetically to hundreds of Iraqi soldiers who simultaneously surrendered believing being instructed by Allah. The use of technological holograms may also be useful in deception as well.

Other references connecting this technology to the globalization effort, mass population control grid, can be seen in many, many books on this subject, such as *Behold a Pale Horse* by William Cooper in which Cooper writes:

*In mind control, this is accomplished through command repetition or microwave thought transference the information is stored in the membranes of the memory cells for instant recall and will continue to be available until the patterns begin to weaken and the belief system kicks-in and starts overriding the weakening program.*

*Each victim in mind control is constantly monitored, and as a program weakens, it is automatically re-programmed or the victim is placed on "command-as-needed."*

*The key to mind control success lies in the fact that the potential victim will think with sensory data instead of thinking with self-knowledge. No power in the universe can override the thought patterns of self-knowledge. There is no greater protection against mind control than the contemplated intelligence stored in the noetic atmosphere of the brain. We don't have to call on it or even be aware of its existence; the energy of need draws it into action."*

There is a war going on between good and evil on many levels and it is no joke.

As it is above, so shall it be below. However, the power of destiny for humanity will prevail as we continue to recognize real purpose, awaken, the veil lifts, and all illusion dissipates.

Not only will there be government restructuring during this critical period, but also that of ineffective educational structures. Many of which have been put in place, in many cases, as a subtle form of mind control designed to keep humanity in line, and all thinking the same way or uniformly, as exampled by everyone having to take the prerequisite Psychology 101, which fosters not thinking outside the box or expressing the innate creative freedom which has resulted in an inability to access a truthful reality.

One of the greatest humanitarians, of all time,

Mahatma Gandhi had this to say in various quotes:

1. "God has no religion"

2. "I am Moslem, Hindu, Christian, Buddhist and Jew. And so are you."

3. "You must be the change you want to see."

Regarding brotherly love and the advancement out of the first three dimensions of consciousness and into the fifth, I believe Gandhi's Law of Our Species is relevant which reads:

*I am not a visionary. I claim to be a practical idealist. The religion of nonviolence is not meant merely for the rishis and saints. It is meant for the common people as well. Nonviolence is the law of our species as violence is the law of the brute.*

*The spirit lies dormant in the brute and he knows no law but that of physical might. The dignity of man requires obedience to a higher law-to the strength of the spirit.*

The lower realm of war must no longer exists! The Rishi of India who discovered the law of nonviolence in the midst of violence were greater geniuses than Newton. They knew the use of arms, then realized their uselessness, and taught a weary world that its salvation lay not through violence but through nonviolence. Violence is a consciousness of fear in the survival mode of the un-evolved operating in the realm of ego driven illusions.

There is no lack or limitation anywhere in the entire Universe. The belief that there is intentionally creates hate towards each other and a false belief that someone is taking something from you when they aren't. There is enough for everyone. This is purely a spoon-fed perception created in the mind by fear and doubt for control.

The spell is broken and the veil is lifting.

We are in the awakening, ascension, evolution, new dimension progression, and the Second Coming.

The doctrine of mystery schools and secret societies using esoteric knowledge for mind control, through religion, education, media, and through the constant promotion of fear for many, many, many, years, will stand no longer.

We now recognize the energy of God as the One and only powerful force for good, behind, and in everything. Knowledge is power and awareness is the key.

The energy of this exhilarating timed ascension has been amped and is working at this very moment for change, and will continue to shatter that which is out of date, with the development of human higher consciousness and a new Earth.

Renee Pittman

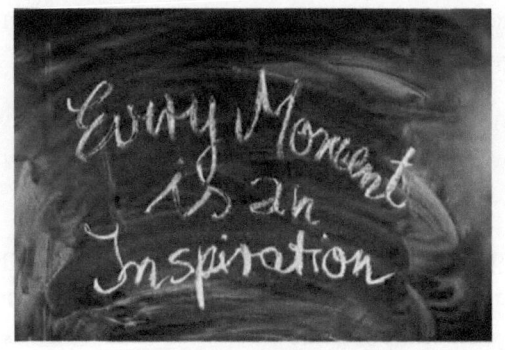

**CHAPTER NINE**

# The Universal Church of God

*"We are all playing our individual roles, working together as part of a larger spiritual team to advance humanity and the world to a more loving and conscious place. To do so, the old ways must be challenged and weakened."*

~ Renee Pittman

The Universal Church was the original name of the Roman Church in the second century. It must be understood that I explore is the authentic Church of God.

The term "Catholic" is itself derived from the Greek word katholikos meaning "universal". The Catholic Church draws its primary values from the Catholic Bible. These 73 books of supposed sacred scripture is made up of the Old Testament and the New Testament in combination and are believed to have been handed down since the time of the Apostles. Today this church continues to fall due to hypocrisy. The energy of change has begun.

The modern-day Universal Church was founded on the core tenet of right and wrong, however it has expanded its view to encouraged increased ecumenism, and even interfaith dialogue. The Universal Church of today advocates for cooperation and understanding among the many faiths of the World. However, many ask is the concept yet another covert method of the One world governance goals.

The Universal Church's motto is despite our differences "We are all children of the same universe."

Today, the manifestation of the Universal Church is simply the acknowledgment of the church within each of us, the love that binds us in Heart, and our resulting efforts of action and service not only directed at each other, but all, to include our earthly home, Mother Earth. It is the church of love and respect for all life, animals, plants, and a determination that our actions mirror and magnify universal intent.

It is not a concept many believe of another effort for control by global evil doers and their relentless hope for "One World Governance." Nor will, ultimately, this concept be accepted by the awakened.

We are the drop of water never disconnected from the whole and we are the rays that shoot outward in expansion like the Lotus, and an expression of the originating Source which again is not a man.

This revelation should bring great peace and release each of us from the bondage of fear which has ensured "divide and conquer" and again, the spoon-fed delusion that there is lack and limitation of Earth.

It should motivate humanity to put down weapons of mass destruction, work together, compromise and grow.

It should motivate to clothe the poor, eliminate starvation and poverty, house the homeless, accessing the creator energy within our hearts and minds.

As a reflection of our creator, these traits are natural to us as we come to remember, why we are really here, who we really are, and are no longer deceived by the deceptive material or physical nature on earth's school or the controllers. After all, did not Satan and his crew fall down to earth?

When we do, open our eyes, through clarity, it inevitably is a new day.

Renee Pittman

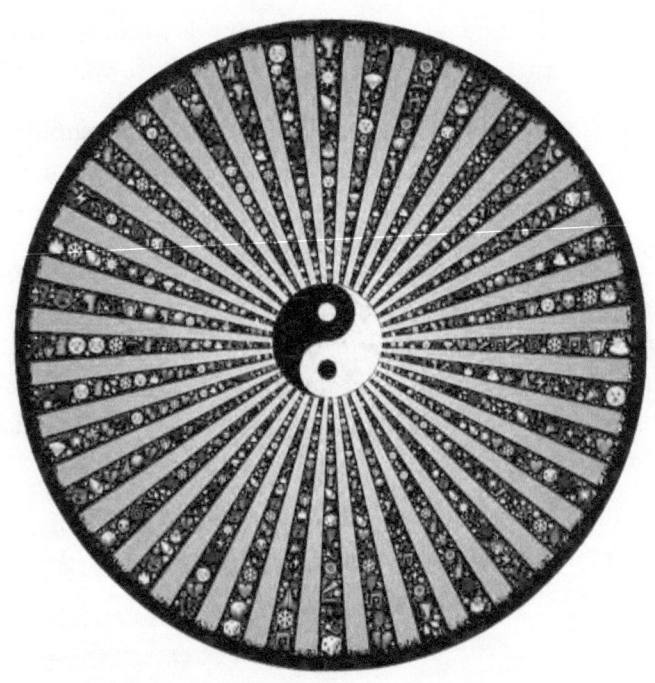

**CHAPTER TEN**

# Nobody Told Me the Road Would be Easy

"Becoming enlightened, but still far to go, I awaken from the dream.

I think, "wow, what an amazing God!" and when it is all said and done, "What an amazing life!"

What a magnificent grand plan God has for each of us recognized as the truth and awareness of that which God has created remains immortal and infinite and that death is a lie and the soul progression is real to higher heights.

Through the illusion of mud or the base of growth for the Lotus, reflected as struggles on the material plane, consciousness expands assuring fulfillment of a masterful plan which has set the stage for step-by-step growth, development, and ultimate enlightenment.

What a wonderful, powerful, God, co-creating with us, allowing free will, and always loving us unconditionally, when we fall, and even when there is temporary blindness, on our path, or when we take a wrong path. When it is all said and done, in the end, it is all good and it's all God!

As Co-Creators within the universe, and the understanding that we can really create only good, and that we are here for God, and acceptance that all experiences resulting in igniting this reality becoming knowledge of the profound "I AM" as the energy inherent in all of life, our view of life changes.

Life then becomes the sacred playground of amusement and joy on the path as it is meant to be.

In doing so, we no longer experience pain though misinterpretation resulting from vital experiences, or belief in separation from God or fear of each other or the world itself.

We are the Lotus regenerating and making the ascension upwards, towards the Universal Light Force of God day after day, for growth, from the mud, has now freed us from the illusion of the muddy bank of the Delta and a false reality.

As we grow in stages of life, advancing from a consciousness similar to infancy to adulthood, on this physical plane, experiences become blessings.

Keep your head up!

We each are destined to blossom in the fullness of glory and *Divine Consciousness* at our appointed time no matter what mistakes we make, how many times we have to restart the journey, again, and again, as necessary until we get it right.

Do not forget or despair and always remember that unconditional love is at the foundation of it all by loving design.

You are well loved under all circumstances.

Part of our mission is accomplished with this understanding and acceptance of new beginnings redirects our path in the value of it all as God's highest creation.

Look no further. Look within. God lives within the Heart!

Remember, "Nobody said that the road or your chosen path or mine would be easy".

As we meditate in this light and awareness, the acceptance of a greater understanding unfolds.

We are transformed knowing that it is by our Will that we may have even selected the path, for growth, development and what we needed to learn.

With knowledge of our ultimate goal, identity and destiny, and the goal of the hopeful return to the Garden of Eden meaning an Edenic state, the journey of our soul, through it all, makes complete sense and there is no longer doubt, fear, pain, sorrow or confusion.

Kahlil Gibran said:

*We choose our joys and sorrows long before we experience them.*

Recognize that the path we each take is designed to bring us back ultimately home and into the fullness of light.

How can we not be thankful for it all?

As for me, I humbly drop to my knees in desire for this light to consume me, to continue to light my way.

I raise my hands toward the infinite heaven and acknowledge that there is no greater honor or greater glory than to bow and kneel before God's Universal Throne.

Altruistic desire and intent in our heart is always God tapping at the door of our consciousness, with infinite supply.

Just continue to put one foot in front of the other.

Be aware that we have the power to dissipate and change our reality by changing our thought process, and beliefs with practice to break the programming, and by also transmuting darkness and negativity into Light. And as a perfect and beneficial form then to be used for the highest good.

Know that we have the ability to consciously cleanse, clear, balance, harmonized and attune ourselves within the metaphysical Green Healing Light and the Golden Light of Grace and be renewed each and every day.

Do not waver, change or doubt this and faithfully declare it as reality.

This is the symbolic ability to move mountains.

The mountain may not have actually moved, it just does not exist for us anymore as an obstacle in our minds.

When we learn of this great and powerful capability, individually and collectively, and each set our hearts and minds to create a beautiful world, when our contract has expired, we leave behind a powerful legacy on this planet.

After mastering this transformation, our soul individually and collectively, spiritually, will continue on to the next lesson in eager anticipation.

However, if we are stubborn, or we just don't get it, or are motivated by the lower realm of self, we will continue to experience the same scenario over and over again, with the same outcome, repeating itself until we do as a trap.

I hope that each and every soul that holds this book in their hands, will take it as food for thought and begin to lift thoughts out of the lower vibration and begin to co-create with universal good intent and become determined to consciously create only goodwill on this planet, no matter what.

Let us all let the thought of being a beneficial presence on the planet resonate within our hearts, minds and souls.

Love is all that matters and, in this consciousness, now awakened, we become the true expressions of the Spark of Divine Light within illuminated originating by a heart's desire.!

The Heart is another Name for God

*"Equal to the breath-spirit of another, the soul-self we think of as separate but which the womb of the Holy One includes, you, I and all humanity, as the First Child of Eden."*

~ Author Unknown

"The poet Rumi reminds us, "**You are not** a **drop** in the **ocean; you are the entire ocean** in a **drop**." For any of us to make peace with and respect the individuality of the others is **not** possible if **we** do **not** accept and make peace with own individuality ... and our individual struggles and triumphs."

*Never forget we can have many new*

*beginnings in this amazing lifetime!*

# OTHER BOOKS BY RENEE PITTMAN

**The "Mind Control Technology" Book Series**

- ❖ Remote Brain Targeting
- ❖ You Are Not My Big Brother - Menticide
- ❖ Covert Electronic Murder: Pain Ray Beam
- ❖ Diary of an Angry Targeted Individual
- ❖ "The Targeting of Myron May – Florida State University Gunman: Asst. DA Pushed Over the Edge
- ❖ Deceived Beyond Belief: The Awakening - Prologue

These nonfiction books can also be accessed at the website below with further details on mass, social and population control technology.

http://www.bigbrotherwatchingus.com

Email the author at: love.energyunited@live.com

**LIVE LOVE ENERGY**

www.ingramcontent.com/pod-product-compliance
Lightning Source LLC
Chambersburg PA
CBHW030911080526
44589CB00010B/255